Lov
YA

John

Shag's Little Book of Love

SHAG'S
Little Book of
LOVE
Dating, mating, and mischief making

Eve Lederman
Illustrated by Shag

Surrey Books
CHICAGO

Meeting Mr. Right

VOLUNTEER AT A HOSPITAL

The cute guy recovering from the quadruple bypass is a captive listener.

TAKE A YOGA CLASS

Show off all your poses
and stretches. Or just
wear a turban and look
cool. Either way, you'll
stir up some interest.

BROWSE THE BAKERY AISLE

All those cherries and frosting and gooey chocolate fudge. In your most sugary voice, tell the guy in line you prefer to wear your whipped cream because you're lactose intolerant.

DONATE BLOOD

Pretend to faint so he can hold you up and then chat over the free juice and cookies while you're recovering. There's nothing sexier than a good Samaritan, and why not let someone else ask all those embarrassing disease-related questions for you.

GO TO A PERSONAL GROWTH SEMINAR

Break down. Cry. Expose your inner child. Latch onto a co-dependent who wants to be the magical solution to all your problems.

First Date Do's and Don'ts

7 DO ASK HER IF SHE ENJOYED THE EVENING AT THE WRESTLING MATCH

8 DON'T COMPLIMENT HIS TOUPEE

9 DON'T STROKE HER WATTLE

10

DO USE THE WORDS
"BREATHTAKING,"
"STARLIGHT,"
"HEAVEN" AND
"ANGEL"

11

DON'T USE THE
WORD "FECAL"

12

DON'T SAY, "I'M KIND
OF SEEING SOMEONE"

13

DON'T ITEMIZE
THE BILL

It's All About Timing

WHEN TO SAY "I LOVE YOU"

When she's swinging a bat at your Ferrari
When your tourist visa expires
When her father answers the door
with a rifle
When you wake up with a ring
on your finger

WHEN NOT TO SAY "I LOVE YOU"

When you're in bed with her best friend
To get the remote back
When your sports team wins
When you mean "I love you naked"
When you're seeing double

Instant Love Letter

CHOOSE A WORD TO FILL IN THE BLANKS AND VOILÀ—AN INSTANT LOVE LETTER THAT WILL MAKE YOUR MATE SWOON (OR SMACK YOU UPSIDE THE HEAD).

My sweet little _____,
jailbait, leprechaun, larva

Your eyes sparkle like _____
rain drops, tinfoil,

_____ and I drink in your
cubic zirconium

smile like _____. The
fine wine, Gatorade, barium

first time we _____,
kissed, played twister, got arrested

I knew I'd want to be with you

until _____.
eternity, tomorrow morning, you're broke

I can't stop thinking about your

_____, and when you
body, rich parents, big screen TV

_____ across the room, my
tap dance, sashay, twirl

_____ starts to _____.
heart, ganglion, lumbar region   sing, tango, purr

You are more beautiful than _____
words, my ex,

_____ and when we are together I get that
my mother

_____ feeling in my _____
queasy, fervent, tingly   gut, big toe, goiter

that tells me you're my _____.
angel, first cousin, nemesis

Your lips are ruby red like _____
a baboon's behind,

_____, your skin as smooth
your bloodshot eyes, a hematoma

as _____. You are as
a used car salesman, Brillo, an oil slick

precious as _____ and
pocket lint, a tax refund, plutonium

I dream about you during every _____
commercial,

_____. I can't live without
AA meeting, night in jail

your _____. Will you be my
love, trust fund, bad breath

_____?
Valentine, lap dancer, Green Card sponsor

Easy Personal Ads

HERE ARE SOME TIPS TO ATTRACT THE LOVE OF YOUR LIFE. IF THEY RESPOND. DO A BACK-GROUND CHECK.

DON'T LIE, EMBROIDER

5 foot 4 is not "statuesque."

199 pounds is considered below 200 only if you are a professional wrestler.

"Athletic" means more than a daily walk to the doughnut shop.

"Rubenesque," however,
sounds exotic.

"Curvaceous" connotes
femininity.

"Husky" is strong and
masculine, as if you could
protect your date from a
grizzly attack, should it
be necessary.

Bald, however, is bald.

LIE BY OMISSION

If you don't have a job,
say you are a free spirit.
If you are wanted by the
FBI, describe yourself
as a buccaneer.
If you live with your
mother, call yourself
a family man.

LEAVE ROOM FOR A LITTLE MYSTERY

Don't divulge everything up front.
Wait till the second date to show
off your yodeling. Better yet,
wait till you're married.

SPEAK TO YOUR AUDIENCE

If you want a "Hot babe to pleasure me for a night of debauchery," you need to ask for a "Mature woman to love me for a lifetime of adventure."

USE KEY RELATIONSHIP WORDS

Describe yourself as emotionally available. Talk about your desire to be vulnerable and emotionally honest, and to share your inner self. Chicks gobble that stuff up.

Five Guys to Avoid

THE NEW AGER

This man wears magnets in his
shoes and he's more in touch with your
feelings than you are. He does Reiki and
Rolfing and by your third date he'll be
dragging you along to seminars called
"Let Go and Live" (as opposed to "Hold On
and Die"). You'll never get a good meal
out of this man unless you like
your food irradiated.

THE WEIGHT LIFTER

He is all muscle and not much else, as all blood flow is usurped by his biceps. He spends more time on the scale than you do and dumps protein powder on everything you cook. On a positive note, he makes you look at least 20 pounds lighter than you really are.

THE BEER DRINKER

This guy will insist on having a keg at his wedding. He has a beer can permanently glued to one hand so he can only participate in a limited range of activities which preclude washing dishes, taking out the garbage or doing laundry.

THE WHINER, A.K.A. THE MOMMA'S BOY

This fellow carries a lunch pail.
You have to loosen lids for him.
He calls you to help move furniture.

When you get together with his
family, his mother will occasionally hold a
kerchief up to his nose and say "blow."
Twenty years from now you'll be cutting his
food and testing his coffee on your wrist.

THE FIXER UPPER

If you could just wax his chest, cut his hair and put him on a lifting routine he'd be perfect. At which point he'll run off with a Victoria's Secret model.

Getting to Know You

ARE YOU TALKING TOO MUCH? NOT ENOUGH? MUMBLING? LISPING? STUTTERING? SLURRING? SIT BACK. TAKE A DEEP BREATH AND FOLLOW THIS EASY LIST OF SUGGESTIONS FOR CAREFREE CONVERSATION.

ASK BACKGROUND QUESTIONS

Where were you born? Where did you go to school? Do you like to torture small animals?

ASK THOUGHTFUL QUESTIONS

What are your hobbies?
Who are your heroes? Would you rather
be mauled by a wild boar
or buried alive?

ASK SEXY QUESTIONS

Are you ticklish? Do you like kissing
in public? Have you ever done it
with your cousin?

CLARIFY ISSUES THAT ARISE DURING THE EVENING

"You mentioned living in exile for a few
years . . . how did that come about?"
"I couldn't help but notice you have an
oxygen tank strapped to your back . . .
tell me more."

TALK ABOUT THE WEATHER

Not a rising barometer, but something juicy.
Has there been an exciting natural disaster
lately? Was your house demolished
by a tornado? Car sucked away by a
mudslide? Sharing personal trauma
is a bonding experience.

"Real Life" Dates

ONCE YOU'RE PAST THE FIRST COUPLE OF DATES, YOU'LL WANT TO SEE HOW YOU FUNCTION AS A COUPLE. DO YOU WORK TOGETHER AS A TEAM? CAN YOU DEAL WITH DIFFICULT SITUATIONS AND MAKE AGREEABLE DECISIONS? TRY THESE REAL-LIFE ACTIVITIES TO TEST YOUR LONG-TERM POTENTIAL.

GO SWIMMING

It's a great way to see someone naked without seeing him naked. You can scout for excess body hair, claw-like hangnails, third nipples and fins.

GO GROCERY SHOPPING

If you can grab the coffee while he looks for the bread and meet back at the bananas in five minutes, you're well on your way to compatibility.

DO LAUNDRY TOGETHER

Does he know to separate the
whites or does he stare at the machine like
it's a space craft? Have his briefs shredded
down to the size of a molecule? Are there
any strange garments in his bag—
pantyhose in his size?

TAKE A WALK THROUGH THE LATE-NIGHT PART OF TOWN

Does he put his arm around you and hold
you close? Does the scantily clad woman
on the corner call out his name?
Hand him change from last week?

That Relationship Talk

THERE COMES A POINT IN EVERY RELATIONSHIP WHEN THE WOMAN WANTS TO KNOW.

"WHERE IS THIS GOING? HOW SERIOUS ARE WE? ARE WE PLANNING A FUTURE TOGETHER?"

SPEAK HIS LANGUAGE

Wear that black lacy number and serve him beer and chips. He'll be putty in your hands. Be specific. Men do not understand allusion, innuendo or metaphor. They know nothing of subtlety which is why they yell out "nice rack" to anyone on the street with a short skirt. Tell him you want a one-and-a-half-carat princess cut diamond ring in a size six with VS1 clarity set in white gold by midnight on December 31. Or else you'll smash his car to smithereens.

DON'T USE "YOU" STATEMENTS

"You self-centered, pig-headed, lying, cheating, brainless, spineless toad . . ." Not productive—unless you are wearing a bikini, in which case he probably didn't hear you.

REMOVE ALL DISTRACTIONS

Men have 3o% fewer connections between the right and left sides of their brains than women, which means they can only perform one task at a time. That's why he tells you to be quiet when he's looking for the highway exit.

Are you in Love?

TAKE THE QUIZ,
ADD UP THE POINTS.
IF IT'S SEVEN OR LESS—
TAKE THE LAST
CHAPTER TO HEART.

When you're kissing, do you think about

a) big, ugly, crusty cold sores
b) replacing the kitty litter
c) breathing in his soul

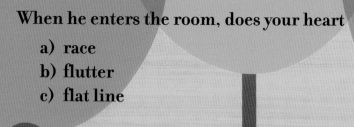

When he enters the room, does your heart
  a) race
  b) flutter
  c) flat line

The last fight you had with your boyfriend was about
    a) who won the last fight you had
    b) geopolitics in Burma
    c) whether he should get chest implants

If you were grounded on a plane with him for five hours, would you
    a) hijack the aircraft
    b) lock yourself in the bathroom
    c) lock yourself in the bathroom with him

When you're both 80 years old, can you imagine

   a) feeding him applesauce
   b) sailing around the world
   c) mud wrestling

What is your boyfriend's favorite hobby?

   a) tinkering with cars
   b) tinkering with you
   c) macramé

What is his most annoying habit?

   a) breathing
   b) biting your nails
   c) flirting with your mother

Give yourself one point for "a," two points for "b" and three points for "c."

0-7: Congratulations. You couldn't have picked a worse mate. Lose him now before you wake up in a trailer with eight kids, two teeth and no husband.

8-14: You get along great but have all the chemistry of a second grade science project. You'll get married and move into a split level ranch house in a neighborhood with good schools. While you're pruning the rhododendrons on a Wednesday afternoon he'll empty the bank account and take off with his secretary. You'll lose the house and start hitting the bourbon hard, trying to find chemistry in the back of dark bars at the fading age of 40.

15-21: He is your true love and soul mate, a man who has captured your heart like no other.

Breaking It Off

IT'S OVER. END OF STORY. SAYONARA. NOW YOU JUST HAVE TO LET HIM KNOW WITHOUT HURTING HIS SENSITIVE, ELECTRON-SIZED EGO.

LEAVE THE DOOR OPEN

"I'm considering thinking about the possibility of the responsibility of a commitment at some future point in time. But until then let's see other people."

TAKE RESPONSIBILITY

"You are the most revolting, despicable creature I've ever known and I curse the day I first laid eyes on you. But it's not you, it's me."

CONFUSE HIM
"I just don't feel what you felt
when we discussed how you thought
you said you felt when I felt that
we're not right together."

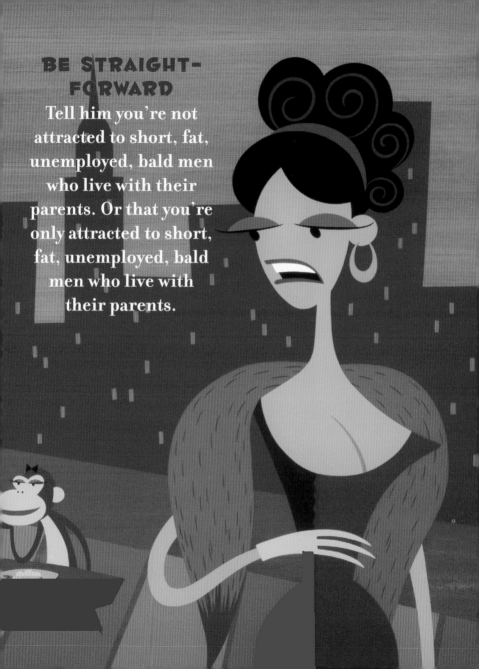

BE STRAIGHT-FORWARD

Tell him you're not attracted to short, fat, unemployed, bald men who live with their parents. Or that you're only attracted to short, fat, unemployed, bald men who live with their parents.

SHAG'S LITTLE BOOK OF LOVE
is published by Surrey Books, 230 E. Ohio St., Suite 120,
Chicago, IL 60611.

Illustrations by Shag
Text by Eve Lederman
Designed and typeset by Joan Sommers Design, Chicago
Printed and bound in China
  by C&C Offset Printing Co., Ltd.

5 4 3 2 1

Library of Congress Cataloging-in-Publication Data

Lederman, Eve
  Shag's little book of love : dating, mating and mischief making /
Eve Lederman ; illustrated by Shag.
     p. cm.
   ISBN 1-57284-079-X
   1. Courtship—Humor. I. Shag. II. Title.
  PN6231.C66L44 2005
  818'.602—dc22   2004022654

Distributed to the trade by Publishers Group West.

www.surreybooks.com
800.326.4430